martinis

martinis

ben reed

photography by william lingwood

RYLAND
PETERS
& SMALL
LONDON   NEW YORK

Senior Designer Susan Downing

Editor Miriam Hyslop

Production Patricia Harrington

Art Director Gabriella Le Grazie

Publishing Director Alison Starling

Mixologist Ben Reed

Stylist Helen Trent

First published in the United States in 2003
by Ryland Peters & Small, Inc.,
519 Broadway
5th Floor
New York NY 10012
www.rylandpeters.com

10 9 8 7 6 5

Library of Congress Cataloging-in-Publication Data

Reed, Ben.
  Martinis / Ben Reed ;
        photography by William Lingwood.
      p. cm.
Includes index.
  ISBN 1-84172-384-3
  1. Martinis. I. Title.
  TX951 .R35524 2003
  641.8'74–dc21
                              2002013055

contents

introduction

What is a martini? To many drinkers it can only be one thing: gin and vermouth with either a lemon zest or olive garnish. If this were the case and the boundaries for producing a martini were this rigid, we would not have the variety of "martinis" that we enjoy today.

The argument of how best to make a martini is an outdated one. There are any number of ways to make a classic martini—all depend on personal taste (and how can that be a bad thing?). The trend of calling any drink prepared using gin or vodka as a base and served in a martini cocktail glass a "martini" is, I think, what infuriates the purists. Just between you and me, I take secret pleasure in defying these sticklers for tradition. Indeed, I go so far as to pounce on such dinosaurs with a war cry of "try a Cheesecake Martini on for size!"—less to influence opinion than to check that they are still awake!

I've categorized these drinks into groups to give you an idea of the differences in the ways they are made. Some require a little bit of preparation, others rely on the freshest, ripest fruit; for others still, the most delicate touch of an added ingredient is what lends the drink its individuality.

Taking ideas from cocktail bars around the world, along with a healthy smattering of my own creations, I've put together a list of martinis that should delight and amaze but, most important, add a little color to the cheeks! You'll find that it's a wide-ranging collection—some you will love, some you may hate, but that's the whole fun of cocktails. There's a cocktail for everyone, and once you find it, you're well on the way to a drop of enlightenment.

martini basics

TECHNIQUES The three basic methods used to make a martini are **stirring**, **shaking**, and **pouring** (also called the diamond method). Each method, performed correctly, has a direct effect on the character of the drink and the way it appears in the glass.

Stirring Place a barspoon into a mixing glass and fill it with ice. Stir gently in a continuous motion until the glass is cold to the touch. Add a dash of vermouth and stir (each stir should last for about 10 revolutions—try to avoid chipping the ice, which dilutes the martini) before discarding the dilution and the vermouth. Finally add the liquor and stir.

Shaking Add the ingredients to a shaker and fill it with ice. Shake with strong, sharp movements (remembering to keep a hand on both parts of the shaker!). This method is useful when you mix creamy martinis.

Pouring (or **diamond method**) For the coldest, purest martini—simply place a bottle of gin or vodka and your martini glasses in a freezer for 6 hours. To serve, add a dash of vermouth to a chilled glass, swill it around, and discard. Pour the frozen liquor into the glass for an unadulterated cocktail.

EQUIPMENT For a "stirred" martini you will need a **mixing glass** with a **strainer**. A **cocktail shaker** is essential for those who prefer their martinis "shaken." One with a lid and a strainer is ideal. You will also need a **jigger**. Modern jiggers are the most useful as they measure both 1 oz. and 2 oz. (a double and a single measure). A long-handled **barspoon** is useful for stirring drinks and "muddling" or crushing fruit, herbs, etc.

GARNISHES The traditional garnishes for a martini are of course an **olive** or a **lemon twist**. A certain amount of poetic license can be used when creating garnishes for newer cocktails. Your choice of garnish should complement both the taste and the appearance of the drink. A **lemon zest** (or **twist**), properly prepared and added to the surface of a classic martini, transforms the drink. Take a sharp knife and gently skim a length of peel from the lemon—the zest should be fine with no pith. Squeeze the zest over the drink, wipe it around the rim,

and then drop it into the liquid. Another type of lemon garnish is the **lemon peel**—simply slice a thin peel from a lemon and drop it into the drink. For a **flaming orange zest**, take a thick orange zest and squeeze it, skin down, over a flame and the surface of the drink (the juice from citrus fruit is flammable); then drop the zest into the martini. Another simple and effective way to garnish your martini is to "**rim**" the glass with cocoa powder, salt, or nutmeg. To do this, wipe a piece of orange around the rim of the glass and place the glass rim down in the powder, creating a neat rim around the edge. Make sure the powder does not mix directly with the martini.

classic

As any mixologist worth his salt will tell you, there's very little point in experimenting with modern cocktail variations unless you know your classics. The recipe for the classic martini, despite being strictly adhered to in certain circles, is also one of the most dabbled-with recipes in the history of the cocktail. The classic martini has evolved, in keeping with social tastes, into the ultra-cold, ultra-dry, predominantly vodka-based cocktail enjoyed today.

classic martini

This is how I would make a "standard martini"
for anyone who asked for one. While the
pouring or diamond method (see page 8)
is faster and the resultant drink stronger
(less diluted), stirring the cocktail is a more
authentic method and the original labor of love
for any bartender.

a dash of vermouth (Noilly Prat or Martini Extra Dry)
3 oz. freezing gin or vodka
an olive or a lemon twist, to garnish

Add both the ingredients to a mixing
glass filled with ice and stir. Strain into
a frosted martini glass and garnish with
an olive or a twist. Alternately use the
diamond technique.

gibson

The leading theory behind the origin of this classic martini is that it was first made at the beginning of the 20th century for Charles Gibson, a famous illustrator, at the Players Club in New York. Whatever its roots, this classic drink has truly withstood the test of time.

a dash of vermouth (Noilly Prat or Martini Extra Dry)
3 oz. freezing gin or vodka
a cocktail onion, to garnish

Add both the ingredients to a mixing glass filled with ice and stir. Strain into a frosted martini glass and garnish with a cocktail onion.

gimlet

A great litmus test for a bar's cocktail capability—
too much lime and the drink turns sickly, not enough
and the drink is too strong. This one needs to be
shaken hard to guarantee a sharp freezing zestiness.

1 oz. Rose's lime cordial
1¾ oz. gin or vodka

Add both the ingredients to a shaker filled
with ice, shake hard and strain into a frosted
martini glass.

dirty

This martini is also known as the FDR, after the man
who called an end to Prohibition in the '20s. Fittingly,
the great president was an accomplished bartender
who loved nothing more than flourishing his shaker
for any head of state with a like mind or a dry palate.

a dash of vermouth (Noilly Prat or Martini Extra Dry)
3 oz. freezing gin or vodka
a large dash of brine from the olive or onion jar
an olive, a twist of lemon, or a cocktail onion, to garnish

Add all the ingredients to a shaker filled with
ice, shake sharply, and strain into a frosted
martini glass. Garnish with an olive, a twist
of lemon, or a cocktail onion.

vesper

Named by James Bond in the film *Casino Royale*—
Bond christened the drink he devised after his
Bond girl de-jour Vesper Lynd. A shaken, medium-
dry concoction.

2½ oz. gin
1 oz. vodka
½ oz. Kina Lillet (French vermouth)
a long lemon peel, to garnish

Add all the ingredients to shaker filled with
ice, shake, and strain into a frosted martini
glass. Garnish with the lemon peel and serve.

montgomery

This martini is named after Field Marshall Montgomery, an Allied hero of World War II. Considering "Monty" fought in the North African desert, it's surprising that he didn't prefer something less dry!

1 part vermouth
15 parts gin or vodka
an olive or a lemon zest, to garnish

Stir all the ingredients in a mixing glass filled with ice and strain into a frosted martini glass. Garnish with an olive or lemon zest.

horse's

This recipe stems from the days when gin and vodka were considered medicinal. The ginger would have been added not only to flavor the elixir, but also to act as an herbal remedy to cure most ills.

½ oz. ginger liqueur

2 oz. vodka

a whole lemon peel, to garnish

Add both ingredients to a shaker filled with ice, shake sharply, and strain into a frosted martini glass. Garnish with a whole lemon peel.

martinez

The Martinez is believed to be the first documented martini, dating back as far as 1849, when it was mixed for a miner who had just struck gold in the town of Martinez, California. Its sweet flavors were geared to appeal to the taste buds of the time and the availability of certain liquors.

2 oz. Old Tom Gin
½ oz. sweet vermouth
a dash of orange bitters
a dash of maraschino
a lemon twist, to garnish

Add all the ingredients to a shaker filled with ice, shake, and strain into a frosted martini glass. Garnish with a lemon twist.

the personaltini

As a lover of martinis of all shapes and sizes,
I didn't find it easy to name my favorite, but
here it is. A naked black Stoli martini, stirred
and served up. Create and name your own
martini.

2½ oz. Stolichnaya vodka
a black olive, to garnish

Add the Stoli vodka to a mixing glass
filled with ice, stir until the mixing glass
frosts, and strain into a frosted martini
glass. Garnish with a black olive.

the ultimate

Every martini should be made using
the very finest components. Make this
martini the "ultimate" by choosing from
the exceptional quality alcohol now available.

1 drop Vya dry vermouth
2 oz. freezing ultra-premium gin or vodka
a twist of lemon or an olive, to garnish

Rinse a frosted martini glass with
the vermouth and discard. Add the
liquor and garnish with a twist of
lemon or an olive.

fresh+fruity

The fresh and fruity martini started as a back-lash against the prevalent cocktail movement of the '80s—that of sticking a chocolate bar into a bottle of vodka for a few weeks and trying to drink the resultant sludge. Rather than rely on various drinks manufacturers to create credible fruit-flavored vodkas, we (the cocktail cognoscenti) decided to regulate the flavors and the concentration of our own martinis. By simply macerating the freshest, ripest fruit with vodka or gin in a shaker, you, too, can create an irresistible martini.

pomegranate

Because this is one of the subtler of the fruit martinis, you must make sure the pomegranate is ripe. Try to avoid getting any of the fruit's bitter pith in the drink, as this would destroy its delicate balance.

2 oz. vodka
1 pomegranate
a dash of simple syrup
pomegranate seeds, to garnish

Spoon the pomegranate "flesh" into a shaker and crush, using a muddler or the flat end of a barspoon. Add ice to the shaker with the remaining ingredients. Shake sharply and strain into a frosted martini glass. Garnish with a few pomegranate seeds.

23

cherry

This martini can also be made using
the juice from canned cherries—it may
not sound as nice but wait until you taste
it. For a delicious variation, try using the
juice from tinned lychees—another winner!

3 stoned fresh cherries
2 oz. vodka
2 oz. thick cherry juice
a dash of cherry schnapps

Crush the cherries in a shaker.
Add ice and the remaining ingredients,
shake sharply, and strain into a frosted
martini glass.

pear

This fruit martini is certainly not for the faint-hearted. Unlike a lot of the fruit martinis, whose sweetness belies their strength, this one pulls no punches.

2 oz. vodka
a dash of Poire Williams eau de vie
a thin pear slice, to garnish

Shake all the ingredients in a shaker filled with ice and strain into a frosted martini glass. Garnish with a thin slice of pear and serve.

raspberry

The raspberry is an old favorite of mine.
This martini should be fairly thick in
consistency, so if you aren't using purée,
use a handful of raspberries to make sure it
flows down your throat like molasses.

2 oz. vodka

a dash of framboise

a dash of orange bitters

½ oz. raspberry purée

2 fresh raspberries, to garnish

Shake all the ingredients in a shaker filled
with ice and strain into a frosted martini
glass. Garnish with two fresh raspberries.

french

The French martini is great for parties since it is light and creamy, and simple to make in bulk. Shake this one hard when preparing it, and you will be rewarded with a thick white froth on the surface of the drink.

2 oz. vodka

a large dash of Chambord
(or crème de mure)

3 oz. fresh pineapple juice

Add all the ingredients to a shaker filled with ice, shake sharply, and strain into a frosted martini glass.

citrus

Another old favorite, the citrus needs to be shaken hard to take the edge off the lemon. Try substituting lime for lemon for a slightly more tart variation.

2 oz. Cytryonowka vodka
1 oz. lemon juice
1 oz. Cointreau
a dash of simple syrup
a lemon zest, to garnish

Add all the ingredients to a shaker filled with ice, shake sharply, and strain into a frosted martini glass. Garnish with the lemon zest.

fresca

The Fresca was invented to be served long with lemonade as a refreshing summer drink, but for every drinker that wants their thirst quenched, there will always be two who want their socks knocked off—and who am I to argue? See opposite for a choice of ingredients.

Add the ingredients to a shaker filled with ice, shake sharply, and strain into a frosted martini glass. Garnish and serve.

basil and honey fresca

2 oz. vodka

a dash of lime juice

a dash of grapefruit juice

2 sprigs of basil, crushed

a teaspoon of honey

a basil leaf, to garnish

orange and pear fresca

2 oz. vodka

a dash of lime juice

a dash of grapefruit juice

a slice of orange, crushed

a slice of pear, crushed

an orange zest, to garnish

port and blackberry fresca

2 oz. vodka

½ oz. port

a dash of lime juice

a dash of grapefruit juice

six blackberries (two to garnish)

red snapper

The Red Snapper was the name given to the Bloody Mary in the 1940s when the original name was deemed too risqué for American sensibilities at the St. Regis Hotel in New York. We've taken the name and changed the format—make sure this one is extra spicy.

2 oz. Old Tom gin
3 oz. tomato juice
spice mix:
    4 dashes of tabasco
    a pinch of celery salt
    2 dashes of lemon juice
    a pinch of ground black pepper
    4 dashes Worcestershire sauce
black pepper or lemon zest, to garnish

Add all the ingredients to a shaker filled with ice, shake sharply, and strain into a frosted martini glass. Garnish with a sprinkle of black pepper or a lemon zest.

gazpacho

This savory drink might sound like a
strange choice, but, trust me, it works!
The Gazpacho came about when a friend
and I went out for brunch and were
looking for a change of drink from the
Bloody Mary. Gazpacho was on the menu,
so we put two and two together—et voila!

2 oz. pepper vodka
black pepper
1 cup gazpacho soup
chopped herbs, to garnish

Shake all the ingredients really hard
with ice and strain into a martini
glass. Sprinkle on some chopped
herbs to garnish.

strawberry

Use the ripest strawberries in this martini. The strawberry flavor is enhanced by a dash of fraise (strawberry liqueur), but it should be kept to a minimum compared to the fresh fruit.

3 fresh strawberries
2 teaspoons simple syrup
2 oz. vodka
a dash of fraise

Place the strawberries in a shaker and muddle with the flat end of a barspoon. Add the remaining ingredients, shake hard and strain into a frosted martini glass.

basil grande

One of the few martinis that doesn't contain
vodka as a base. Expect lots of strong flavors
in this extravagantly fruity concoction. It's a great
alternative to creamy cocktails after dinner.

4 strawberries (one to garnish)
2 basil leaves (one to garnish)
2 oz. Grand Marnier
1½ oz. Chambord (or crème de mure)
3 oz. cranberry juice

Crush the strawberries and the basil leaf
in a shaker. Add the remaining ingredients
with ice, shake sharply, and strain into a
frosted martini glass. Garnish with a strawberry
and a basil leaf.

35

pontberry

The Pontberry martini is a snip to prepare since it involves no fresh fruit. Strong and sweet, it should appeal to a wide range of palates.

2 oz. vodka
3 oz. cranberry juice
a large dash of crème de mure

Shake all the ingredients in a shaker filled with ice. Strain into a frosted martini glass and serve.

blood martini

A bittersweet concoction that needs to
be delicately balanced. The lime and
the Campari provide the bitterness, while
the sweet element comes in the form of
the raspberry liqueur. Taste the drink
before and after adding the orange zest—
what a difference!

2 oz. vodka

1 tablespoon Campari

2 teaspoons framboise

1 teaspoon fresh lime juice

2 tablespoons cranberry juice

a dash of Cointreau

a flaming orange zest, to garnish

Add all the ingredients to a shaker
filled with ice, shake sharply, and
strain into a frosted martini glass.
Garnish with a flaming orange zest
(see page 9).

gotham

As sinister and mysterious as the name
suggests. Try varying the amount of black
Sambuca (one of the most underused cocktail
ingredients I know) for a darker, more
threatening result.

2½ oz. frozen Stolichnaya vodka
a dash of black Sambuca

Pour the vodka into a frosted martini glass,
gently add the Sambuca, and serve.

clean+serene

"Clean and serene" martinis are designed for those of us who still enjoy the clarity and the purity of the classic, but appreciate an added touch of spice. They smooth and caress the taste buds with the same poetry of the originals, while delighting the senses with a hint of something extra. From the Thunderer with its perfumed touch of lavender, to the Gotham and its subtle traces of aniseed, these cocktails convey the elegance and sophistication of the classic martini with the added allure of extra taste.

thunderer

This cocktail smells almost perfumed.
A hint of Parfait Amour—a beautifully
named orange curaçao flavored with violets
—and a tease of cassis is all this drink
needs to achieve its flowery, distinctive taste.

1¼ oz. frozen vodka
2 drops of Parfait Amour
2 drops of cassis
2 blueberries, to garnish

Pour the Parfait Amour and cassis into
a frosted martini glass. Add the frozen
vodka and garnish with two blueberries.

applejack

Taken from recipes using American apple brandy, this concoction relies heavily on the addition of Manzana apple liqueur, a green apple liqueur that lends a bitter-sweet quality to the martini.

1 oz. vodka

1 oz. Manzana apple liqueur

1 scant oz. Calvados

a thin slice of apple, to garnish

Add all the ingredients to a mixing glass filled with ice, stir until the glass appears frosted, and strain into a frosted martini glass. Garnish with a thin slice of apple.

joe average

Despite its name, there is nothing average about this drink. Nor should the Pimm's in the recipe fool you—this is not a drink to be taken lightly!

2¼ oz. Stolichnaya vodka

a dash of Pimm's No. 1 cup liqueur

a thin slice of cucumber and a lemon
**   zest, to garnish**

Add the ingredients to a mixing glass filled with ice, stir until the glass appears frosted, and strain into a frosted martini glass. Garnish with a thin slice of cucumber and a lemon zest.

legend

Invented in London in the late '80s, this
recipe has to be followed closely because too
much of any of the ingredients can result
in an unpalatable cocktail. Make sure you
taste each concoction before you serve it.

2 oz. vodka
1 oz. crème de mure
1 oz. fresh lime juice
a dash of simple syrup

Add all the ingredients to a shaker filled
with ice, shake sharply, and strain into
a frosted martini glass.

decadent

To the old-fashioned martini drinker, there is no time or place for the more elaborate new concoctions. Yet with a martini—as with anything important in life—I believe there's room for a little poetic license. If the drink tastes amazing and maintains the level of elegance expected from a martini, then as far as I'm concerned, there's not a problem!

orange brûlée

The Orange Brûlée is a dessert drink that should be savored. You'll notice I don't recommend the caramelization process— would you trust a bartender with a blowtorch?

1 oz. Grand Marnier
1 oz. Amaretto
a dash of white crème de cacao
whipping cream, to top
thin strips of orange zest, to garnish

Add all the ingredients except the cream to a shaker filled with ice, shake sharply, and strain into a martini glass. Whip the cream and dollop it gently onto the surface of the drink. Crisscross with orange zest.

claret cobbler

The Claret Cobbler has long proven to be
a classic that can take whatever time throws at it.
The combination of fresh citrus juices, raspberry
liqueur, and port or claret* may even have the
wine buffs sitting up and paying attention …

one lemon slice

one lime wedge

one orange wheel

2 tablespoons claret or port

1 oz. vodka

1 oz. framboise

Muddle the fruit in a shaker. Add the
remaining ingredients, shake sharply
and strain into a frosted martini glass.

* Red Bordeaux or Cabernet-Merlot blends.

black bird

The Black Bird isn't a spur-of-the-moment type of drink. The work put in beforehand is in equal proportion to the look of amazement on its drinker's face. The Cointreau and the brandy in the mix draw all the juices out of the berries, and they combine with the alcohol in a most un-alcoholic way. One to be wary of.

1 oz. lemon juice

4 teaspoons Cointreau

berry mix*

   ½ cup strawberries

   ½ cup raspberries

   ½ cup blueberries

   ½ cup cranberries

   1 oz. brandy

   1 oz. Cointreau

   1 lb superfine sugar

   2 oz. lemon vodka

Place a scoop of berry mix into a frosted martini glass and press down. Pour the remaining ingredients into a shaker filled with ice, shake sharply, and gently strain the mixture into the martini glass.

To make the berry mix, add all the ingredients to a container, stir once, and leave overnight. Stir once more before serving.

hazelnut

This martini has proven popular with men and women alike. A strong, clear chocolate martini with an undercurrent of hazelnut, perfect for after dinner with coffee—dessert and a nightcap rolled into one.

2 oz. vodka
4 teaspoons crème de cacao (light)
2 teaspoons Frangelico (hazelnut liqueur)
nutmeg powder (for the rim)

Add all the ingredients to a shaker filled with ice, shake, and strain into a frosted martini glass with a nutmeg rim.

black bison

The central ingredient in this mix is Zubrowka,
a vodka that tastes of freshly cut hay, and lends
a distinct quality to any cocktail. Combine this with
Chambord (a black raspberry liqueur from France's
Loire Valley), and you have a truly memorable union!

2 oz. Zubrowka vodka

4 teaspoons Chambord (or crème de mure)

½ oz. fresh lime juice

a dash of simple syrup

4 black currants (or blueberries)

one blueberry, to garnish

Muddle the fruit in a shaker. Add the
remaining ingredients to the shaker with
ice, shake sharply, and strain, into a frosted
martini glass. Garnish with a blueberry.

cheesecake

You'll need a spoon with this one—
it's effectively an alcoholic dessert.

graham cracker
2 teaspoons simple syrup
2 oz. vodka
½ oz. Chambord
½ oz. raspberry purée
½ oz. heavy cream

Grind the cookie into crumbs, add
the syrup, mix, and pack everything into
the bottom of a martini glass. Add the
remaining ingredients in to a shaker,
shake and strain gently over the crumbs
into the martini glass.

turkish chocolate martini

I've always wanted to find a credible drink that includes rose-flower water, and here it is. The heaviness of the crème de cacao combines with the lightness of the flower water to create a truly Turkish delight!

2 oz. vodka
2 teaspoons crème de cacao (light)
2 dashes of rose-flower water
cocoa powder (for the rim)

Add all the ingredients to a shaker filled with ice, shake, and strain into a frosted martini glass with a cocoa rim.

lemon meringue

When set the challenge to create something special with Drambuie Cream, I thought I'd bend the rules a little. Mixing citrus fruits with cream liqueurs generally isn't recommended for cocktails, but somehow this concoction resists the temptation to curdle.

2 oz. Cytryonowka vodka
4 teaspoons lemon juice
½ oz. Drambuie Cream
a dash of simple syrup

Add all the ingredients to a shaker filled with ice, shake sharply, and strain into a frosted martini glass.

ginger cosmopolitan

A superb variation on one of the great modern classics. The trick is to get the amount of ginger just right. The mix of flaming orange zest, ginger, lime juice, and lemon vodka gives this drink an incredible depth of taste.

2 oz. lemon vodka
½ oz. triple sec
½ oz. fresh lime juice
1 oz. cranberry juice
2 thin slices of ginger
burnt orange zest, to garnish

Add all the ingredients to a shaker filled with ice, shake sharply, and strain into a frosted martini glass. Garnish with a flaming orange zest.

classic cosmopolitan

Sex and the City made this drink popular,
its great taste ensured it stayed that way.

2 oz. lemon vodka

½ oz. triple sec

½ oz. lime cordial

1 oz. cranberry juice

Add all the ingredients to a shaker
filled with ice, shake sharply, and
strain into a frosted martini glass.

herbed+spiced

The infusing process requires a little extra effort, but prepared with proper care and attention, these cocktails will bless the drinker with that timeless quality of the classic martini. While this procedure may overlap in some people's minds with buying preflavored vodka, remember that the person doing the infusing (that's you) holds all the cards. If you are creating chile vodka with habañero chiles, it is your decision to maim or merely incite! Place the bottle in a cool environment to infuse in a refined and delicate manner, or for a quicker, more brutal method of infusion, the liquid should be left somewhere warmer.

hibiscus

It's always worth experimenting with the Hibiscus before you serve it to your guests, as the concentration of the juice can vary—overdo the hibiscus if in doubt.

1 oz. vodka

a dash of lime juice

a dash of framboise liqueur

2 oz. hibiscus cordial*

  2 cups sugar

  ¼ pound hibiscus flowers

  1 quart of water

an hibiscus flower or petal, to garnish

Add all the ingredients to a shaker filled with ice, shake sharply, and strain into a frosted martini glass. Garnish with a hibiscus flower.

To make the cordial, dissolve the sugar and hibiscus flower into a quart of water on a low heat. Once the liquid turns deep red, strain and leave to cool.

cowboy hoof

Who knows where the name for this minty special originates! The color of the drink alone is worth the effort. Do pay attention when straining the mixture—bits of mint sticking to the teeth is never a good look.

12 mint leaves
2 teaspoons simple syrup
2½ oz. gin
a sprig of mint, to garnish

Shake all the ingredients in a shaker filled with ice and strain into a frosted martini glass. Garnish with a sprig of fresh mint.

lemon grass

A gentle hint of lemon grass is all that is
needed for this concoction to work. Try
this martini before sitting down to a Thai
meal. The lemon grass skirt in the photo
is not a recommended garnish (unless you
have a degree in basket weaving.)

1½ oz. lemon grass-infused vodka*
3 sticks of lemon grass (one to garnish)

Add the vodka to a mixing glass filled
with ice, stir until the glass is frosted,
and strain into a frosted martini glass.
Garnish with a thin slice of lemon grass.
* *Place two split lemon grass sticks in
a bottle of vodka and leave to infuse for
two days.*

elderflower

Elderflower cordial has become a
must-have on bar shelves in recent
years—try this recipe with gin instead
of vodka as a base, and marvel as the
juniper and other flavorings in the gin
combine with the sweet elderflower!

2 oz. vodka
1 oz. lime juice
½ oz. elderflower cordial
a dash of simple syrup
a dash of orange bitters
a lime zest, to garnish

Add all the ingredients to a mixing
glass filled with ice, stir until the glass
is frosted, and strain into a frosted
martini glass. Garnish with a lime zest.

cajun

A word of warning, this drink must be monitored while it is infusing. Habañero chiles are among the strongest in the world and should be treated with respect. A glass of milk will neutralize the effect.

2½ oz. habañero-infused vodka*
4 habañero chiles (one to garnish)

Add a large measure of vodka to a mixing glass filled with ice and stir until the glass is frosted. Strain the mixture into a frosted martini glass and garnish with an habañero chile.

* Place three habañero chiles (with seeds) in a bottle of vodka and leave until they start to loose their color (the more translucent they become, the more flavor has been absorbed).

tokyo

This martini can be a bit scary if it is made badly. Try to find the best-quality wasabi and the freshest ginger.

2 oz. gin
2 thin strips of fresh ginger
a small roll of wasabi
ginger strip, to garnish

Add the ingredients to a shaker filled with ice, shake, and strain into a frosted martini glass. Garnish with a thin strip of ginger.

red star

Unlike the Licorice Martini, the Red Star is a delicate drink. Make sure the glass is well frosted to highlight the hint of aniseed taken from the seed of this Chinese plant.

2 oz. vodka

1 tablespoon star anise-infused dry vermouth*

2 star anise (one to garnish)

Add the dry vermouth and the vodka to a mixing glass filled with ice and stir until the glass is frosted. Strain into a frosted martini glass and garnish with a star anise.

* Infuse one star anise in a bottle of vermouth (Noilly Prat) for two days.

licorice

For a stronger flavor, or if you're in a rush, pop the licorice into a bowl of vodka and place it in a microwave on full power for two minutes. Admittedly, it's not a natural thing to do because it does burn off some of the alcohol, but if you want to cut corners …

2½ oz licorice-infused vodka*
a dash of Pernod
2 strips of licorice (one to garnish)

Pour the vodka into a shaker filled with ice and shake sharply. Rinse a rocks glass with a dash of Pernod and discard the liquor. Fill the glass with ice. Strain the mixture into the glass and garnish with a strip of licorice.

* Add a 4-in. strip of black licorice to a bottle of vodka and leave for half an hour.

index

CONVERSION CHART

Measures have been rounded up or down slightly to make measuring easier.

Imperial	Metric
½ oz.	12.5 ml
1 oz. (single)	25 ml
2 oz. (double)	50 ml
3 oz.	75 ml
4 oz.	100 ml
5 oz.	125 ml
6 oz.	150 ml
7 oz.	175 ml
8 oz.	200 ml

ACKNOWLEDGMENTS

A big thank you to all of the team behind the mixologist. Most notably to William Lingwood, his ability to bring drinks to life is second to none. Thanks to Helen Trent, whose enthusiasm is bettered only by her eye for objets d'art.
Much appreciation to Alison for excelling in her role as my literary mentor, and thanks also to Miriam and Susan, for putting in all the real hard work.
Mostly, thanks to my mum for all the obvious reasons.
The author and publisher would like to thank the following companies and stores who loaned materials for the book:
The Conran Shop +44 (0)20 7589 7401; Fandango +44 (0)20 7226 1777; Harvey Nichols +44 (0)20 7201 8584; Heal's +44 (0)20 7636 1666; Pullman Gallery +44 (0)20 7930 9595; Thomas Goode +44 (0)20 7499 2823; and Undercurrents +44 (0)20 7251 1537.